Space & Solar System Singalong to the tune of B...

13 Planets
for children

How to say the tricky names:

Ceres (Seer-reez)
Haumea (How-may-ah)
MakeMake (Makkee-Makkee)
Eris (Ear-riss)
Kuiper (like wiper or piper)

Look out for me on every page as I will set you puzzles and challenges!

Some of them are rocky, some are balls of gas. Come learn about their temperature, orbit, moons and mass.

Grey, grey Mercury, the closest to the Sun.

It is the hottest planet at 900 Fahrenheit.

Blue, blue planet, home to us earthlings.

Are there more birds or clownfish?

Earth has the perfect atmosphere to support living things.

We call it the red planet as its iron turned to rust.

Grey, blue Ceres, I was an asteroid.

How many red stars?

A dwarf now as my shape's unique, it's called oblate spheroid.

It's more than twice the combined mass of planets round our star.

Jupiter is so big it has at least 79 moons!

My Earth-like moon called Titan, could develop living things.

The gas giant Uranus, has the perfect name you'll see.

So far away my orbit takes sixty thousand days!

Pluto was a main planet, a dwarf now as it's small.

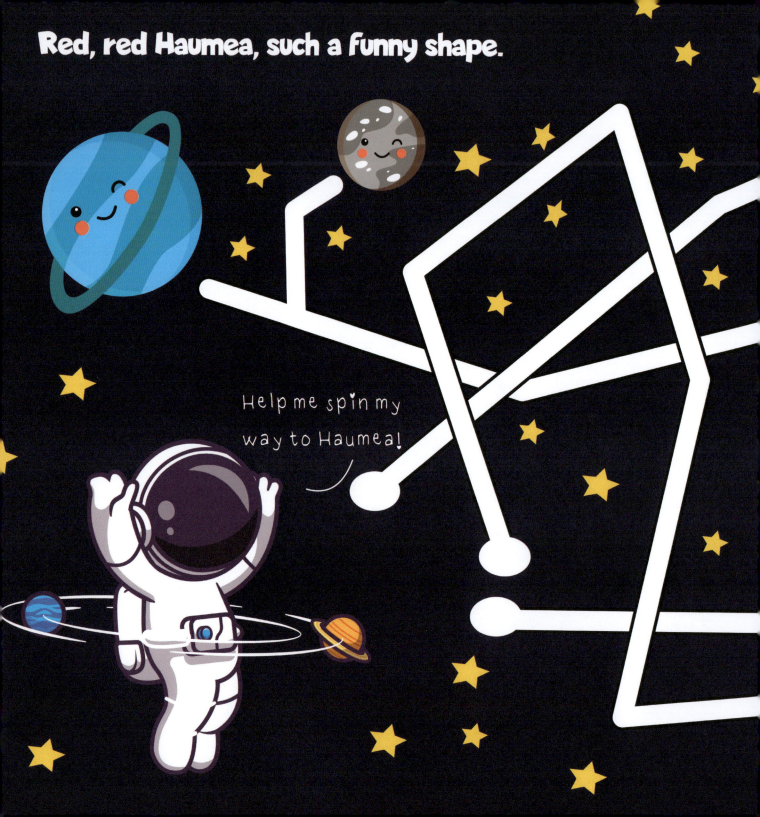

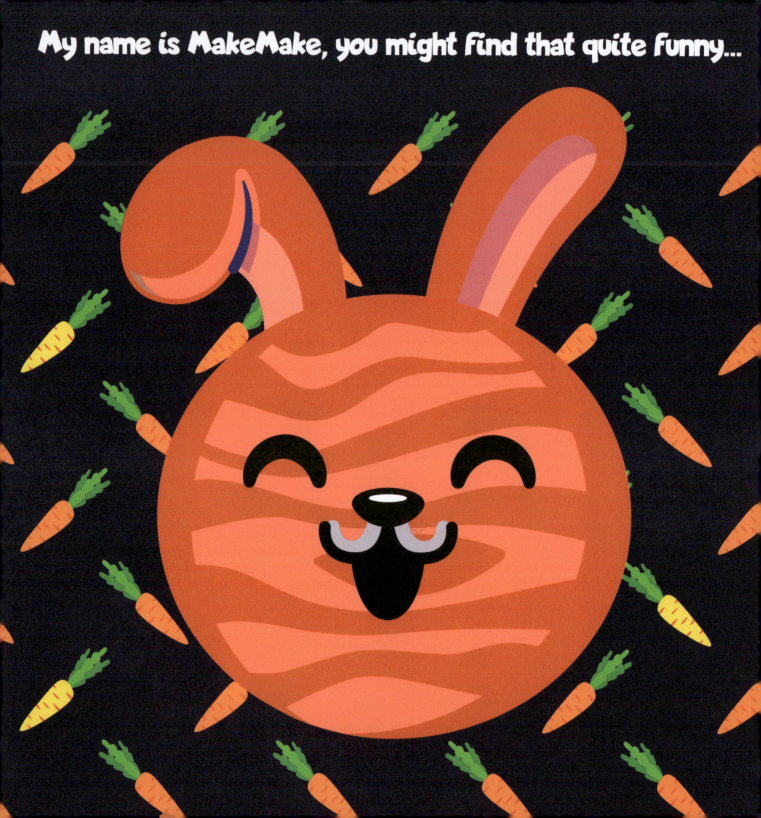

Far, far Eris, bigger than Pluto.

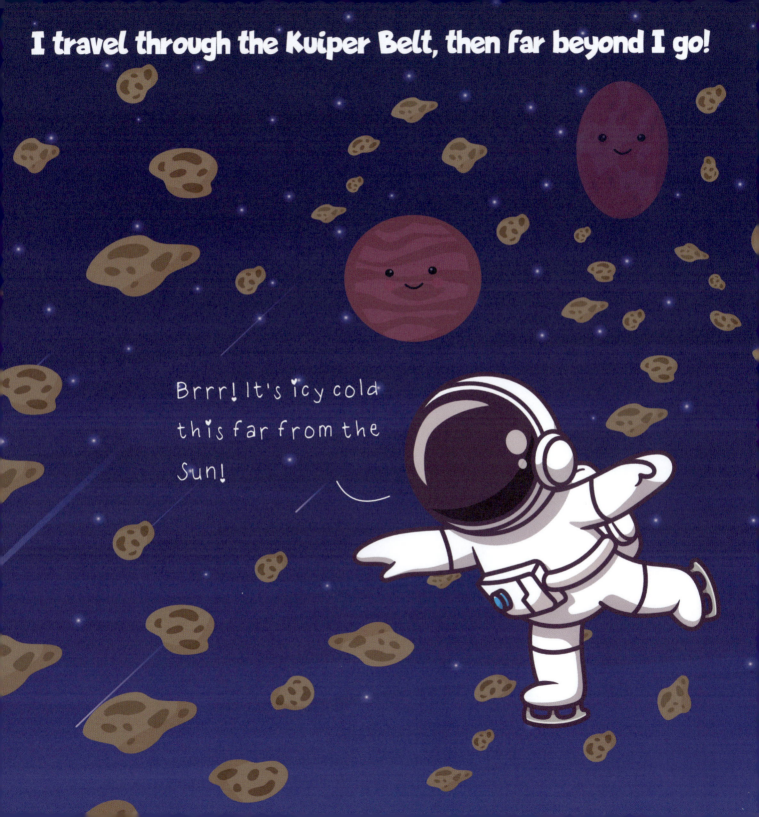

13 planets, all bid you farewell.

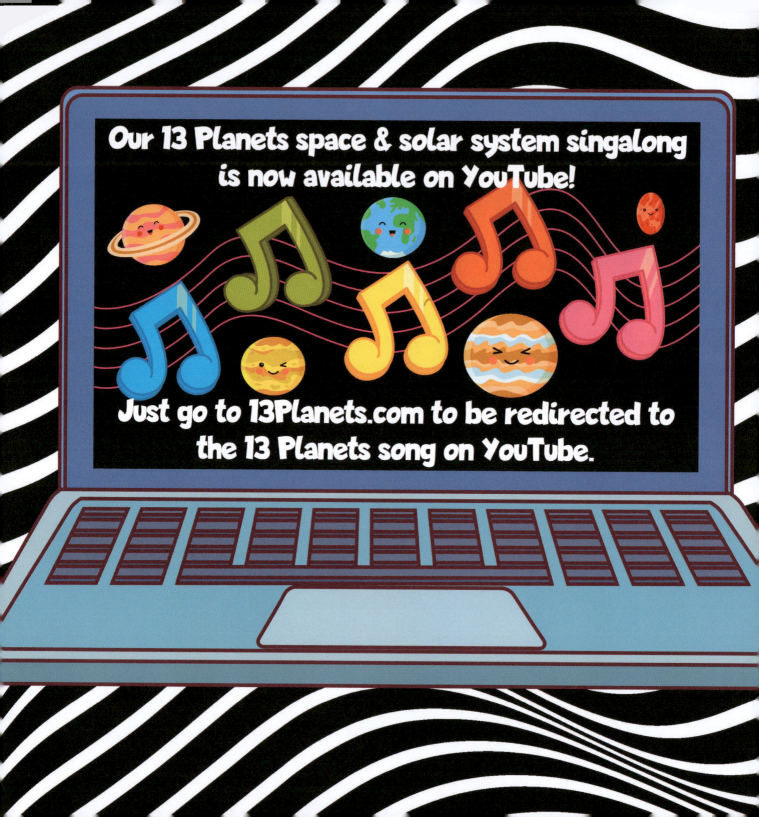

I hope you enjoyed our book! Here are some of our other books that we think you may like too! Just visit us.toomi.biz for Amazon.com or uk.toomi.biz for Amazon.co.uk

Here is a small selection of pages from our best-selling, full colour high definition photo, Car Parts ABC for kids!

See our entire ABC for kids! range on Amazon.

Aa Alternator
It supplies electricity to the car and maintains the charge in the battery.

Bb Brake Rotor
A key component of the braking system that is subject to friction heat.

Ss Shock Absorbers
They create a comfortable journey by preventing spring motion through a process known as dampening.

Tt Turbo
Exhaust gas driven turbine which sucks in air, forcing it into the cylinders, increasing engine efficiency.

Ee Engine
The main source of power. It burns fuel to produce mechanical power.

Ff Fuel Pump
Transfers fuel from the fuel tank to the carburetor.

Qq Quarter Panel
Body part between a rear door and trunk, usually wrapping around the wheel well.

Rr Radiator
It cools the engine by allowing the heat in the coolant to pass to the air outside.

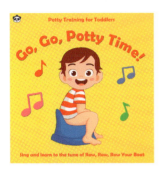

A potty training singalong your little one will love! A step-by-step guide to potty training to the gentle tune of Row, Row, Row Your Boat.

Also includes a full 6 weeks of pre-potty and potty training progress charts!

The perfect bedtime book - A huge array of exciting vehicles with a rhyming story to the tune of the classic lullaby, Twinkle, Twinkle Little Star.

Also includes 16 separate vehicle-based activities, more than many dedicated activity-only books!

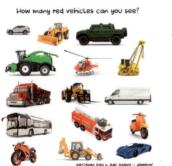

Printed in Great Britain
by Amazon